Wittgenstein's Rhinoceros

Wittgenstein's Rhinoceros

Narrated by
Françoise Armengaud

Illustrated by
Annabelle Buxton

Translated by
Anna Street

Plato & Co.
diaphanes

A little old man with a red tie and a tall young man with a wide-collared shirt are turning over all the tables and chairs of a classroom, one by one. Are they looking for something?

Suddenly, the older one stops short and says with an
irritated tone:
"Mister Wittgenstein, let's get this over with. And look at me,
please! You have been following my logic and mathematics
courses, and I have found that your writings up until now
demonstrate a certain maturity. But right now you are wasting
our time with such childishness! There is no rhinoceros in this
room, admit the obvious!"
"Professor Russell, I'm not joking! How can we say that something doesn't exist and be certain that what we say is true?
I can say, 'A great professor is in this room,' and that is certainly
accurate, regardless of your size, if you'll excuse me... But when
I say, 'There is no ghost here, or treasure, or rhinoceros,' in fact
I don't really know: it's just that I don't see any!"
"Wittgenstein, you drive me crazy... Stop pretending to look
for a horned beast in the very middle of Cambridge University,
or I'll have you sent back to your native Austria! Go away and
don't come back until next week and until then, try and get
some fresh air!"

Upon leaving the classroom, Wittgenstein finds
his friend David Pinsent waiting for him.
"It sure took you long enough!" his friend complains.
"You didn't happen to see a rhinoceros come out of the
room before me?"
"Pardon?"
"Russell claims, just like that, without any reason at all,
that there are no rhinoceroses in Cambridge and advises me
to get some fresh air… Well, I'm going to follow his advice
to the letter. Would you like to take a trip to Iceland?"
"Sure, but I doubt you'll find any rhinoceros over there!"
"Oh, don't you start! Let's go pack our bags and meet
tomorrow at the train station! You'll see, we'll bring
Russell his rhinoceros that doesn't exist…"

Upon arriving in his rooms, Wittgenstein starts packing...
What does one need to hunt an animal that might not exist?
Books? There are many things in books that don't exist while,
at the same time, we can talk about them, and yet not really...

In the end, Wittgenstein stuffs his suitcase with anything and everything within his grasp: books, clothes, souvenirs, the seen and the unseen...
He slams the door on the way out.

He barely makes it a few steps along the street when a horse
and buggy, hurtling by at great speed, almost knocks him over.
On its way, it also frightens a little boy who drops his ball
in the gutter and then bursts into tears.
"My baaaall!"
"We'll find you another one, my dear," consoles the mother.
"All gone my baaaall!

Wittgenstein thinks: "So there you have it,
a blue ball disappears and it's the end of the world!"

"But actually," he says to himself, "it is not the end of the world; it really is the world. What matters is that the ball was in the hand of that child, that his mother was taking him for a stroll, that the horse and buggy went careening by them, and all that. When we speak, we can say whether it's true or not…"

With delight, he takes out his notebook from his pocket and writes down the following sentence:

The world is all that is the case.

The next time he would say to Russell: "Dear Professor, in the world it can always be the case that a rhinoceros may be hiding right where least we expect it."

The two young men meet up at the Cambridge railroad station. While waiting for the train, they browse the shelves of the station bookshop.

All of a sudden, Wittgenstein grabs Pinsent's arm:

"Look at the title of this book!"

"What a coincidence!" exclaims Pinsent, "It is perfect for you!"

Both start to laugh. They purchase the novel of a famous English detective novelist entitled *A Rhinoceros in the Library*.

Wittgenstein is very excited.

"David, listen carefully," he says to Pinsent. "I already have three things to tell you about this rhinoceros:

1) First of all, it inhabits a book: the one written by our famous novelist, a copy of which we acquired. That much is sure.

2) Secondly, it runs, or sleeps, or plays, or God knows what else, in the middle of books, those of the bookshop. This much is sure as well. Do you follow?"

"Yes, Ludwig, I follow!"

3) Finally, this rhinoceros—and this is a question, a major question—, "is it an inhabitant of the world at the same time that it is an inhabitant of a book? And here, nothing is for sure…"

"Ludwig, I don't follow any more, or rather, I don't understand what it is you are trying to say!"

"Too bad for you!"

A loudspeaker announces the imminent departure of the express train for London. "Hurry up," David warns, "or else we are going to miss our train!"

Once they are comfortably seated, Wittgenstein opens his notebook and writes:

Everything that can be thought at all
can be thought clearly.
Everything that can be said
can be said clearly.

He hesitates to add that this doesn't necessarily mean that one is understood!

But he changes his mind and stops writing. Then he gives David, who had begun to sulk, a big smile.

After the train trip, then five days of a difficult crossing during which the two friends suffer from seasickness, they finally arrive in Iceland!

And now, where can a rhinoceros be found in Iceland? Especially if one is looking for a rhinoceros that doesn't exist! In a circus? No, such beasts have never been trained, they only know how to charge—quite dangerous, actually. In a zoo? The last zoo just closed and the next one has not yet opened.

And so there is only one thing left to do: travel up and down the island from high to low, and then some. Speaking of which, a tour guide is offering sightseeing trips, by pony, if you please! The distribution is quickly done: a pony for David, a pony for Ludwig, a pony for the guide, three replacement ponies for when the other three are worn out and two pack ponies for the baggage. Saddle up for adventure among volcanoes, geysers and pastures!

Will there be a rhinoceros upon the horizon?

For the time being, there is no geyser in sight.
No rhinoceros either, but well, that was to be expected.
The little band rides peacefully through the pastures in
the midst of sheep and cows.
David, who is passionately committed to his friend's
hare-brained scheme, cries out while pointing at a large,
horned animal:
"Ludwig, look! There it is, your runaway from Cambridge!"
"My runaway from Cambridge? What do you mean?"
"The rhinoceros, Ludwig, the rhino!"
"But what you are showing me, David, is a bull!"
"Ludwig," David says in a serious voice, "you have to see it
as a rhinoceros!"
"How silly you are, my dear David!"

"Urge your pony forward a little, yes, right there,
now don't move. You can see the bull's profile, can't you?
The two horns now look as if they are one...
and since he is lying down, he is exactly the right size!
Let's sum up the situation: he has the profile of a rhino,
the size of a rhino, and perhaps the ferocity of a rhino
as well!"

Wittgenstein seems to have understood. He starts blinking
his eyes and repeating: now a bull, now a rhino, now a bull,
now a rhino... Then he drops the reins on his pony's neck,
which seizes the chance to nibble on some flowers,
and takes out his notebook. But he finds nothing to write.
Perhaps later he will be able to express this experience.
On the other hand, he makes a suggestion to David:

"Let's call him Rhinobull! A new creature added to the
empire of mythological monsters!"
"Well done, Ludwig, and tonight we will celebrate with
cranberry jam muffins!"

In their room that evening, next to the chimney
and its warm fire, the two young men start playing
snakes and ladders. But Wittgenstein hates this game.
Dice he finds boring. He prefers dominos, and he loves
chess. David, bored by chess, suggests creating a
new counter from a pawn. So he shapes a ball of bread
into a round body. Another, smaller ball on top works
as the head, and the end of a match is stuck into
what could be a snout... Wittgenstein is furious and
reproaches David for making fun of him and of being
obsessed with the rhinoceros.

"Yeah, right," David replies defensively, "as if you aren't obsessed yourself."

"But for me, it's not the same! I am a researcher in philosophy, you see, and... it is imperative that I manage to verify certain things about the rhinoceros. The one you call the Cambridge runaway. As for your poorly-rigged counter, remember that a game is made up of rules and not of pieces in disguise. And if you now start to tell me about the diagonal movement of the rhinoceros, I'll send you straight to the loony bin!"

"And what if I want to call it a rhinoceros?"

"David, there is no such thing as a private language!"

That night, Wittgenstein has a dream. Several times
he dreams the same dream. He is chased by a herd
of rhinoceroses galloping like crazy. From time to time,
he turns around to tell them:
"Calm down! I need only one of you!"
And regularly, the rhinoceroses reply in unison:
"Does it bother you if there are several of us?"

The stay in Iceland is coming to an end. Empty-handed,
Wittgenstein and Pinsent find themselves in Cambridge
for the following semester. It is a rather dull period.
The rhinoceroses all seem to have fled the city. Classes resume.

Wittgenstein has the impression that Russell keeps looking at
him with a mocking eye, even though he doesn't say a word
about the rhinoceros. He eagerly anticipates the next hunting
trip with David. Perhaps in Norway?

Several weeks later, Wittgenstein and Pinsent settle down in the village of Skjolden on the Sogne fjord. They explore the fjord with a small sailboat. Pinsent is steering.

Sitting in the back of the boat, Wittgenstein writes constantly.
Offended that his friend pays him so little attention, Pinsent cries:
"A sea rhinoceros on the port side!"
Wittgenstein shrugs his shoulders and continues working.
Pinsent sighs. Being in the company of a genius has never been
easy for anyone.

Wittgenstein, whose family is far from poor, buys a small piece of land next to a fjord and decides to build a cabin, something that, if not comfortable, would at least be solid, with a door and windows. Not a ramshackle hut.

David mocks him without pity:

"And I suppose you think that once your cabin is finished,
your rhinoceros will come knocking politely at the door,
and you will say to him: 'Come on in, Mister Rhinoceros,
I have been waiting for you, please make yourself at home!'
And then he'll go warm himself by the fire, while you'll offer
him a cup of tea and question him…"

"In your opinion, what will I ask him?" Wittgenstein curtly
interrupts, rather irritated by David's mockeries.

"You'll ask him: 'Dear Rhinoceros, why didn't you show
yourself to Professor Russell in the classroom? You were there,
weren't you? Or were you in fact somewhere else?' And he
will reply: 'Yes, my dear Wittgenstein, I was somewhere else,
I had a cold and had to keep my appointment with the
rhino-logist!'"

Exasperated, Wittgenstein slams the door and takes off
with great strides into the forest. The path leads him far
in the direction of the mountain, surrounded by tall,
dark evergreens and silver birch trees. In some places,
the forest is so dense that the sun's rays barely illuminate
the lichen- and moss-covered ground.

On the other hand, the forest is not so dense:
the combination of beings, animals, things, trees, plants
and humans—not to mention books, which don't exist
in forests—is vast! To constitute an inventory of everything
that doesn't exist would be exhausting. Not even
Wittgenstein would attempt to do it. So, is the sum of
what does not exist in the forest greater than the sum
of what does exist in the forest?

Two squirrels chase each other and scamper down a tree,
dashing like red flames back up the trunk.
If a squirrel could speak, Wittgenstein muses, we would
undoubtedly not be able to understand it. Squirrels,
like all animals, don't have the same experiences that
we have, don't think about the same things, don't have
the same way of life... Moreover, what does it mean to
speak? I am not in an enchanted forest out of a fairy tale...
And yet, fairy tales are trying to tell us something,
but what?

The next day, David prepares breakfast with the treats
he had brought back the previous day from the village.
"Dum dada dum! Announcing that the frokost of
his Highness the Prince of Philosophers is served!
Toast and jam, poached eggs with salad, and little strips
of smoked eel…"

Wittgenstein wonders why his companion is so cheerful.
"It's a morning to celebrate, your Highness!
Listen, Ludwig, I'm on the right track. When you went
to bed, I said to you: 'There is no rhinoceros under your bed.'
Right?"
"So what?" Wittgenstein snaps.
"You see? It was too late! You thought about it! You thought
that there might be one! It bothered you all night! And so,
this morning, I'm telling you: There is no quarrel between
Ludwig Wittgenstein, Prince of Philosophers, and my
humble self. Hmm? Bingo! Too late! You thought about it!
You thought there might be a quarrel, that one was perhaps
already begun… That will bother you for the rest of the day."

"Stop!"

"Tomorrow, you might say to yourself: 'God doesn't exist.'
And bam! It will be too late! It will haunt you for life!
Do you understand?"

"David, what you are talking about belongs to psychology.
It only concerns the things that people have in their head.
That doesn't interest me. What interests me, as you know,
is to see how statements come together with other ones,
some of which can be true together, some of which cannot
be true together… What is it in reality that can make a
statement true or false…? And how can we be sure of its truth
or falsity…? Logic has nothing to do with the imagination!"

"If you and Russell had discovered a rhinoceros under
the table, would that have made you happy?"

"Of course, at least that would have made him understand
the complexity of the problem of a negative fact…"

"So if I understand you correctly, we are not going to take off
on a hunt for crocodiles… No more than on a Snark hunt,
I suppose?"

"David, you know that Cambridge is not responsible for
the menagerie of Oxford!"

"Well," grumbles David, "we still have a rhinoceros on our
hands! Well, no, actually, the little stinker is far from being
within our grasp!"

August 1914. The declaration of war resonates like a thunder clap throughout all of Europe. Vacation is over, childhood is over, or more precisely, the child's play of young, carefree people like David and Ludwig. And worse yet, perhaps the friendship between a young Austrian, whose country is a German ally, and a young Briton, whose country is the enemy.

The time for chasing rhinoceroses appears to be over. Whether or not one exists now seems neither here nor there... or is it still as important?

Wittgenstein enlists in the Austrian army because he loves his country and wants to defend it, and because he wants to prove to himself that he is courageous and is capable of facing death.

He takes his notebooks along because he is determined to continue his work wherever he goes. He hasn't given up. A heading marked 'rhinoceros' is still on the agenda. The problem of the proof of something's non-existence...

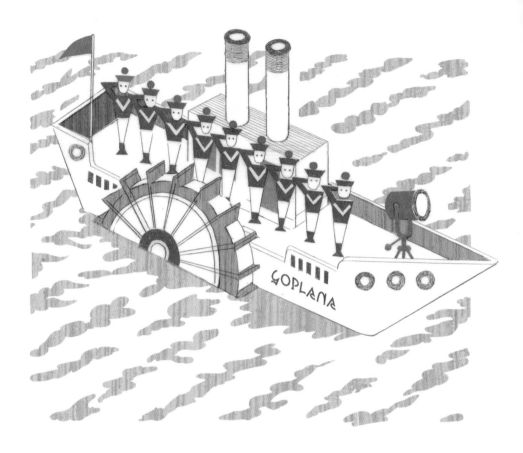

Wittgenstein wonders where he will be sent. The answer comes quickly. He will serve on the *Goplana*, a torpedo boat destroyer recently seized from the Russians. The boat must navigate upstream on the Vistula in pursuit of the enemy. They will not get to see Warsaw or the Baltic Sea, for the simple reason that navigating a river upstream is not as easy as following it downstream. After a few days, Wittgenstein writes his friend.

My dear David,

I didn't expect to have to deal with so much physical hardship.
War is an unpleasant and dangerous ordeal. And we are not
even in the line of fire. But life is difficult on board. On the
boat, we have to sleep in our boots, directly on the floor with
a bit of hay and without any blanket. Outside, the weather
is cold and tempestuous. I read and write on a little wooden
chest. If I am valiant, the reward will be to find at last the
rhinoceros that doesn't exist and to tell its story in the book
that I would like to write.

Ludwig

On the ship's deck, at night, Ludwig must illuminate the riverbanks with a searchlight in order to check whether or not enemy soldiers are waiting in ambush. He is unarmed, but that doesn't prevent him from being in great danger of being killed. Not that he particularly minds, to the contrary. He writes in one of his notebooks:

*"Perhaps the nearness of death
will bring light into life.
God enlighten me!"*

With the searchlight, he can't help but hope to run across a rhinoceros on an evening's stroll. The boat's movements cause the shadowy landscape to appear strange and surreal. Sometimes, in the middle of the reeds, Wittgenstein is surprised by the sudden flight of large aquatic birds which are disturbed by the ship's light. Or sometimes he catches a glimpse of the glowing eyes of nocturnal animals on the run. But as for enemies, none. Certain days, however, the rumbling of nearby cannons can be heard, signaling that battles are being fought.

Finding them too noisy, Wittgenstein does not converse with his comrades on the *Goplana*, but rather writes a lot in his notebook using a code he invented:

"I can die in one hour,
I can die in two hours,
I can die in a month or only in a few years.
I can't know or help or do anything about it:
that's how life is.
How should I live so as to be able
to die at any moment?
Live in the beautiful and the good,
until life itself ceases."

He constantly repeats Tolstoy's words quietly to himself: "Man is powerless in the flesh but free because of the spirit." To live the life of the spirit!

One starry, moonless night, Wittgenstein dreams that his
rhinoceros is transformed into a unicorn. How marvelous!
How splendid! It was an animal that didn't exist and yet
was sought after and loved for its gait, its bearing, its neck,
and even the luminosity of its calm gaze. It received no
nourishment from grain, but only from the possibility
of existing...

Wittgenstein awakes, plagued by a poignant perplexity.
Since it was certainly someone besides himself, who, then,
in the bedazzlement of his dream, could have whispered
to him this yet-to-be-written poem? The legend claims
that the unicorn only lets itself be seen by pure beings.
And he himself, Ludwig Wittgenstein, was he a man of
enough integrity to approach a rhinoceros become unicorn?

How can one trigger a metamorphosis, become another
being, a different individual? Is it through hardship
that one becomes a better person?

The *Goplana* arrives in Cracow, where it berths. A visit of commanding officers is announced to Ludwig. They are accompanied by a man with a strange look about him, who addresses Ludwig with an accent as indefinable as it is suspicious:

"Lieutenant Wittgenstein, your show of courage, endurance and insight has caused you to be recommended for a secret mission in Russia. You must cross the enemy lines without getting caught and, if it's all the same to you, without getting killed. Here is your mission: To provide us with information about the revolutionary upheavals in the country."

Wittgenstein glances over the document, it is signed: *The Rhinoceros who comes from the cold.* He accepts without hesitating.

"Lieutenant Wittgenstein, you are now a member of His Imperial Majesty's secret service. From now on you will only be known as agent number One Two Three Four Five Six Seven. In other words: 1234567. I suppose you can guess why… Yes, we peeked inside your notebook! Our Decryption Department can't make any sense of it, by the way, but now it's your turn: you have one week to learn Russian! And here is the password for when you arrive: *'The most fortunate goose is the Kremlin's yellow rhinoceros.'*"

Disguised as a muzhik, Ludwig leaves Cracow for Moscow hidden in a bale of hay. Jostled around day and night by the train crossing countries of which he sees nothing and knows nothing, he studies his notebook and listens to the conversations.

He is surrounded by grooms who are bringing back retired
artillery horses which have survived severe hardship on
the front. He is cold but very moved to find himself there,
whizzing through Tolstoy's homeland.

Upon his arrival in Moscow, Agent 1234567 surveys Red Square
and stops in awe at the mysterious harmony of the domes
of Saint Basil's Cathedral. Each of the five domes is trying to
say something... But what?

He doesn't have time to pursue his musings because a man
wearing a Russian fur hat comes up to him and whispers hastily
before disappearing:
"Be on your guard! One rhinoceros can hide another."

Then a fat man waddles along in front of him:
"Be careful not to mistake wild rhinoceroses for pioneers
of the Revolution!"

A third individual, smaller than the preceding ones and snug in a blue velvet hood, stops in front of him, holds a folded newspaper up to her face and whispers:

"Who is the most fortunate?"

"The most fortunate goose is the Kremlin's yellow rhinoceros."

"I am your contact, Agent 1234567!" says the small woman who throws back her hood and shows herself to be a ravishing young blond. "Why are you smiling? You know that not everything can be written down for a mission, even a secret one... and not in your notebook either! Follow me."

The world of the happy is quite another
than that of the unhappy.

Following his mysterious guide, Ludwig disappears into the alleys of Moscow until reaching a little room situated across from the entrance to a bustling café where he is requested to monitor the comings and goings of his compatriots. The place bears a strange resemblance to Vienna.

Losing himself in his memories, Wittgenstein takes an imaginary trip to his hometown, Vienna, greeting its familiar beauty and monuments. Next to the Belvedere Gardens, he pictures his childhood home in Alleegasse, which was such an imposing house that people called it the Wittgenstein Palace.

He sees his mother Leopoldine with his sisters
and brothers, who persist in calling him Luki
as they did when he was a kid. Next to a sideboard
covered with cakes and chocolates, under Klimt
paintings and Rodin sculptures, sits his father Karl,
who passed away after a long illness.

The hubbub of the café mingles with the memory of Beethoven sonatas and Brahms' music for clarinet that his mother would have well-known musicians play in the music room. The same piece of music could be interpreted in countless different ways. Ludwig tells himself that understanding a sentence in Russian, or in any language, is not all that different from understanding a musical phrase. If one of the Muscovite café's seated customers, who had no knowledge of what music is, found himself or herself transported to the salon of Wittgenstein's home and heard a meditative piece by Brahms or Chopin, he or she would be persuaded that it was a language, and that the meaning was hidden... Or would he or she rather find themselves like a rhinoceros in a china shop?

Гав Гав

Germany and Austria are almost defeated. Soon, the war will be over. Ludwig, who has received orders to return, is captured on the border by Italian soldiers. To his great despair, they seize his notebook.

Luck has it that the prisoners' camp to which he is sent, set up within military barracks, has a library which, thanks to the bequest of an old scholar who was the previous colonel's brother, is well-equipped. From then on, Wittgenstein doesn't really think about escaping.

He discovers an ancient thinker, Damascius, who makes a very strong impression on him, as he finds in his writings, across the fifteen centuries that separate them, certain of his own ideas which are to him of the utmost importance. Indeed, Damascius criticized the philosophers of his day at length, because they seemed to him to be wasting their time in vain discourse. He wrote: "What will be the end of these discourses if not complete silence, the avowal that we know nothing of that which we are not allowed to know because it is impossible for us to know them…"

One misty morning, after not sleeping all night, Wittgenstein's thoughts turn to his absent friend:

"David, why did I tell you one day that I was only interested in logic, while this is not true, even if it is my true work, my task in this world, at which I hope I have not failed. But surely you know that this was not my only interest. Have we not often discussed what a happy life was, a calm life, what a good life should be...

I would like to be able to tell you now in person that the solution to the problem of life has been found and that the problem no longer arises. The solution of the problem of life is seen in the vanishing of this problem. It is like asking: What problem? Was there a problem? Where's that?

My dear David, people for whom the meaning of life becomes clear after they have put themselves into question and tormented themselves are incapable of saying of what this meaning consists..."

If the world is everything that is the case, the world's noise
is heard only very dimly in the prisoners' camp, and beyond
this fading noise there is silence. But it is a more profound
and more difficult silence that must be embraced:
a silence that renounces hollow speech and signifies that
some things must not and cannot be said.

It is not easy, but it is important to distinguish between that
of which we can, or cannot, be certain, that which we can,
or cannot, know, that which we can, or cannot, express.
To clarify our thinking and to determine the formulation of
thoughts, such is no doubt philosophy's task. But nothing more.
Beyond this, philosophy has nothing to say. If it breaches the
border by trying to say what can only be shown, philosophy
becomes useless chattering.

The more Wittgenstein meditates, the more he is convinced
that his life reveals itself not by his words, not by what he says
but by his actions, the bad as well as the good. It shows itself
for what it is. The choices that he makes are the only way to
show what has value for him. There is nothing to explain.
Above all, do not try to explain! A happy life justifies itself by
itself, it is the only proper life.

That deserves to be written down in his notebook, but...
whatever happened to his notebook?

The Italian cryptologists were not able to understand the seven
sentences written in his notebook any better than the Austrian
deciphering specialists could. They thus dispatched it by way
of a traveling rhinoceros to their British allies, who in turn
sent it to Cambridge to one of their most brilliant logicians,
none other than Bertrand Russell, Wittgenstein's professor.
And so Russell opens the notebook and deciphers:

"I, Ludwig Wittgenstein,
declare on the first day:
'The world is all that is the case.'
And I am quite satisfied with my declaration."

What did he manage to declare the three days following?
In spite of all his efforts, Russell was unable to decipher
propositions 2, 3, 4 and 6. On the other hand, he believes
he understands the fifth as well as the seventh and last
proposition.

The fifth day, I tackle something
more complicated and I give a definition:
"A proposition is a truth-function of
elementary propositions." And I congratulate myself
on this definition which makes logic the key
to the structure of thought.

The seventh day, I declare a day of rest:
"What we cannot speak about we must pass over in silence."
And I am terribly content with this declaration
which brings an end to my work.

Upon reading this, Russell bursts out laughing.
On the first page of the notebook, he writes:

Pure nonsense, isn't it?

Then he thinks a moment, crosses out what he had just written
and in its place traces this title in capital letters:

TRACTATUS RHINOCERO-PHILOSOPHICUS

French edition
Françoise Armengaud & Annabelle Buxton
Le Rhinocéros de Wittgenstein
Design: Yohanna Nguyen
© Les petits Platons, Paris 2013

First edition
ISBN 978-3-03734-547-4
© diaphanes, Zurich-Berlin 2016

www.platoandco.net
www.diaphanes.com

Layout: 2edit, Zurich
Printed and bound in Germany